World War II

WORLD WAR II IN WESTERN EUROPE

by Ryan Gale

FOCUS READERS®
VOYAGER

www.focusreaders.com

Copyright © 2023 by Focus Readers®, Lake Elmo, MN 55042. All rights reserved. No part of this book may be reproduced or utilized in any form or by any means without written permission from the publisher.

Focus Readers is distributed by North Star Editions:
sales@northstareditions.com | 888-417-0195

Produced for Focus Readers by Red Line Editorial.

Content Consultant: Dr. Gideon Mailer, Associate Professor of History, University of Minnesota Duluth

Photographs ©: Shutterstock Images, cover, 1, 4–5, 7, 11, 13, 23, 27, 39, 40–41, 45; AP Images, 8–9, 14–15, 19, 25, 31, 33, 37, 43; Office of War Information/AP Images, 17; Berliner Verlag/Archiv/Picture Alliance/DPA/AP Images, 20–21; Department of Defense/Department of the Army/Office of the Deputy Chief of Staff for Operations and Plans/Training Directorate/U.S. Army Audiovisual Center/National Archives, 28–29; Berliner Verlag/Archiv/Picture Alliance/DPA/AP Images, 34–35

Library of Congress Cataloging-in-Publication Data
Names: Gale, Ryan, author.
Title: World War II in Western Europe / by Ryan Gale.
Description: Lake Elmo, MN : Focus Readers, [2023] | Series: World War II | Includes index. | Audience: Grades 4-6
Identifiers: LCCN 2022008643 (print) | LCCN 2022008644 (ebook) | ISBN 9781637392874 (hardcover) | ISBN 9781637393390 (paperback) | ISBN 9781637394373 (pdf) | ISBN 9781637393918 (ebook)
Subjects: LCSH: World War, 1939-1945--Europe, Western--Juvenile literature. | World War, 1939-1945--Campaigns--Western Front--Juvenile literature.
Classification: LCC D756 .G25 2023 (print) | LCC D756 (ebook) | DDC 940.54/21--dc23/eng/20220321
LC record available at https://lccn.loc.gov/2022008643
LC ebook record available at https://lccn.loc.gov/2022008644

Printed in the United States of America
Mankato, MN
082022

ABOUT THE AUTHOR
Ryan Gale is an artist and writer from Minnesota. He loves reading and writing about history.

TABLE OF CONTENTS

CHAPTER 1
The Rise of Nazi Germany 5

CHAPTER 2
The Phoney War 9

A CLOSER LOOK
The Battle of the Atlantic 12

CHAPTER 3
German Expansion 15

CHAPTER 4
The Axis Powers 21

A CLOSER LOOK
The Holocaust 26

CHAPTER 5
Europe First 29

CHAPTER 6
Operation Overlord 35

CHAPTER 7
Victory in Europe 41

Focus on World War II in Western Europe • 46
Glossary • 47
To Learn More • 48
Index • 48

CHAPTER 1

THE RISE OF NAZI GERMANY

World War I (1914–1918) devastated Europe. Approximately 20 million people died in the conflict. Cities lay in ruins. The winning side was known as the Allies. This group included Britain, France, the United States, and several other countries. Meanwhile, Germany was on the losing side. The Allies wanted to make sure such a terrible war would never happen again. So, they forced Germany to sign the **Treaty** of Versailles.

The Belgian city of Ypres was one of many cities destroyed during World War I.

The treaty required Germany to accept blame for starting the war. Germany also had to pay the Allies huge sums of money for the damage the war had caused. In addition, Germany had to give up parts of its territory. The treaty also limited the size of Germany's military. This was meant to prevent Germany from starting another war.

Many Germans blamed their government for accepting such harsh terms. Adolf Hitler was one of them. Hitler was a member of the Nazi Party. The Nazis called for Germany to abandon the Treaty of Versailles. In addition, they wanted Germany to expand its territory. Nazis also held

> ## CONSIDER THIS
> The Treaty of Versailles was unpopular with many Germans. How do you think the treaty affected their view of the Allied countries?

▲ Hitler held huge rallies to build support for the Nazi Party's racist ideas.

racist beliefs, claiming that Jews were the enemy of the German people.

The Nazi Party became popular with many Germans. Other Germans opposed the Nazis. However, the Nazis used violence against those who disagreed with them. In 1933, Hitler became the leader of Germany. He quickly put the Nazi Party's plans into action.

CHAPTER 2

THE PHONEY WAR

In the fall of 1939, more than one million German soldiers gathered along the border of Poland. They were part of Hitler's plan to conquer Europe. Hitler had spent several years planning for this moment. He had raised armies and built thousands of tanks and airplanes. This military buildup violated the Treaty of Versailles. But Hitler ignored the treaty.

German dive-bombers played a key role in the invasion of Poland.

On September 1, a German battleship began the attack. It fired on a military fort on the coast of Poland. German soldiers and tanks rushed into the country at the same time. Fighter planes and bombers attacked from the air.

The German invasion was powerful and fast. It came from the land, sea, and air all at once. It was a new type of warfare. The Germans called it blitzkrieg, or "lightning war." The Polish military was no match.

Britain and France were Poland's allies. On September 3, they declared war on Germany. However, they could not send help in time. Germany completed the invasion of Poland in only four weeks.

Most people expected more battles after the invasion. But for the next six months, very little fighting took place. People began calling it the **Phoney** War. However, the Allies and Nazi Germany were already preparing for the next phase of the war.

WESTERN EUROPE (SEPTEMBER 1939)

A CLOSER LOOK

THE BATTLE OF THE ATLANTIC

During the Phoney War, armies clashed just once on land. And there was very little fighting in the air. Some fighting did happen at sea, though. Most of these battles took place in the Atlantic Ocean.

The Allies were not prepared to fight on land in 1939. However, Britain had a powerful navy. So, it attacked German merchant ships at sea. These ships carried food, oil, and other goods Germany needed for the war. Sinking these ships hurt Germany's military by stopping the flow of goods.

Germany responded by attacking Allied merchant ships in the Atlantic. Britain is an island nation. As a result, it needed many ships to bring in food and raw materials. The British navy was not large enough to protect every merchant ship. So, merchants began sailing in large groups

▲ An Allied ship sinks in the Atlantic Ocean after being attacked by a German submarine.

called convoys. Several warships traveled with each convoy for protection. But they were still easy targets for German submarines. Submarines could attack from under the water. Being underwater made the subs harder to spot. By the end of the war, the German navy had sunk more than 2,400 British merchant ships. Most were sunk by submarines.

Fighting on the Atlantic Ocean continued until the end of the war in Western Europe. It came to be known as the Battle of the Atlantic.

CHAPTER 3

GERMAN EXPANSION

The Phoney War ended on April 9, 1940. On that date, Germany invaded Norway and Denmark. German ships landed troops in port cities. Paratroopers, or soldiers with parachutes, dropped in from the air. It was the first-ever use of paratroopers in war. The German blitzkrieg worked. Denmark surrendered in just six hours. Norway surrendered on June 10 after two months of fighting. German losses on land were light.

German soldiers torch a village during the invasion of Norway.

However, the invasions were costly for the German navy. The Allies destroyed several of Germany's best warships. The German navy would never be as strong again.

In 1940, France had one of the largest militaries in the world. A long line of forts and **bunkers** ran along France's border with Germany. This defense was called the Maginot Line. The French hoped the Maginot Line would stop a German attack. However, Hitler simply sent his forces around it.

Germany moved through the Netherlands, Belgium, and Luxembourg. On May 10, German forces attacked all three countries at the same time. Luxembourg surrendered in just one day. German forces captured the Netherlands after five days of fighting. Once again, German paratroopers proved to be highly effective.

⛊ The German army destroyed many buildings during its invasion of Belgium, leaving people homeless.

French, British, and Belgian forces tried to stop the German advance in Belgium. But German forces surrounded them and drove them toward the French coast. The Allies retreated to Dunkirk. This port town lay on the northern tip of France. German forces closed in to destroy the trapped

Allies. But Hitler ordered his army to halt just 12 miles (19 km) from Dunkirk. He decided to let his air force finish the job. He wanted to save his soldiers and tanks for future battles.

However, the German air force could not complete its mission. So, after two days, Hitler ordered his army to move on Dunkirk. The delay gave the Allies time to plan a rescue mission. On May 26, the British navy began **evacuating** Allied soldiers. The water off Dunkirk was shallow. Most ships were too large to reach the shore. So, the navy asked British citizens with boats to help pick up soldiers. Hundreds of people with boats of all sizes joined the rescue mission. They brought the Allied soldiers across the English Channel to Britain.

The rescue mission ended on June 4 when German forces reached Dunkirk. Approximately

▲ Allied soldiers crowded onto boats during the Dunkirk evacuation.

340,000 Allied soldiers made it back to Britain. But more than 100,000 Allied soldiers and thousands of vehicles had to be left behind. They were captured by the Germans. Even so, Hitler had missed a chance to deal a major blow to the Allies. Meanwhile, Belgium had surrendered on May 28. The road was now open to France's capital city of Paris.

CHAPTER 4

THE AXIS POWERS

Benito Mussolini was the leader of Italy in 1940. His political beliefs were similar to those of the Nazis. Germany's military victories convinced Mussolini that Hitler would win the war. So, on June 10, 1940, Italy joined the war on the side of Nazi Germany. The two countries were known as the Axis powers.

Axis forces closed in on Paris. The French gave up the city without a fight. By June 25, France's

Hitler visited Paris after German soldiers invaded France.

government had surrendered to Germany. German troops **occupied** the countries they invaded. Hitler sometimes set up new governments that were friendly to Nazi Germany. These countries were known as puppet states. However, some people fought back. Groups of men and women gathered guns and explosives. They killed German soldiers, destroyed trains, and damaged property. These groups were known as resistance fighters.

After France fell, Britain was the only major Allied power left in Western Europe. Hitler expected the British to seek peace. He did not think they would fight the Axis powers alone. But British Prime Minister Winston Churchill chose to keep fighting. As a result, Hitler began planning an invasion of Britain.

The English Channel separates Britain from the rest of Europe. Crossing an army over the channel

▲ A German bomber flies over London during the Battle of Britain.

would require a large number of ships. Those ships would be open to attack by British forces. So, Hitler's first priority was to destroy the British air force and navy.

The Battle of Britain began on July 10. German planes began bombing British ships in the English Channel. Soon after, they began bombing British bases, airplane factories, and **harbors**. British fighter planes fought back. However, Britain had far fewer planes than Germany did. Britain could not stop the attacks. But British workers on the home front worked day and night to make new planes to replace the ones that were shot down.

By September, Germany still hadn't won control of the skies over Britain. So, Hitler ordered his air force to stop attacking air bases and factories. Instead, he had them attack British cities. Hitler thought that if enough **civilians** were killed, the British would seek a peace agreement.

On September 7, the Battle of Britain ended, and the Blitz began. *Blitz* was short for *blitzkrieg*. For nine months, German planes bombed British cities. They hit the capital city, London, the hardest. To avoid the bombs, many people slept in underground subway stations. Meanwhile,

▲ People take shelter in London's subway tunnels during the Blitz.

many parents sent their children to camps in the countryside, where they would be safer.

Despite the bombing, Britain continued to fight. So, Hitler ended the Blitz in May 1941. He wanted to save his air force for an invasion of the Soviet Union. More than 40,000 British people were killed during the Blitz. Even so, Britain did not give up.

A CLOSER LOOK

THE HOLOCAUST

Nazi soldiers swept through Western Europe in the early 1940s. In the countries that Germany occupied, Nazis rounded up any Jews they could find. Entire communities were put on trains and sent to prison camps in Eastern Europe. Few people survived these camps. Those who did endured brutal conditions.

In 1941, Nazi officials changed plans. They began murdering Jews rather than imprisoning them. The Nazis called their new plan the Final Solution. They built death camps that were specifically designed to kill large numbers of people. Nazi Germany and its allies killed approximately six million Jews during World War II. This event is known as the Holocaust.

Allied soldiers freed the camps in 1945. Many of the Germans who worked at the camps were

▲ At death camps, the Nazis killed people with poison gas and burned their bodies in ovens.

captured. They were later put on trial for their crimes. However, the damage had already been done. Two-thirds of the Jews in Europe had been murdered.

CHAPTER 5

EUROPE FIRST

On December 7, 1941, Japan attacked the US naval base at Pearl Harbor, Hawaii. In response, the United States declared war on Japan. Japan had joined the Axis powers the year before. So, Germany and Italy declared war on the United States.

The United States and Britain fought Japan in the South Pacific. Meanwhile, they had to fight Germany and Italy in Europe. But the Allied

Japanese bombers damaged several US battleships during the attack on Pearl Harbor.

military was not big enough to fight all of its enemies at once. In late December, US President Franklin Delano Roosevelt met with Churchill to discuss war plans. Both leaders believed Germany was the greater threat. So, they agreed on a "Europe first" plan. Most of the US military would help the Allies in Europe. At the same time, a small US force would hold back the Japanese in the South Pacific. Once the war in Europe was over, the Allies would focus on defeating Japan.

On January 1, 1942, 26 countries agreed to work together to fight the Axis powers. Joseph Stalin was the leader of the Soviet Union. He wanted the Allies to take back Western Europe right away. Germany had invaded his country the year before. Stalin believed an Allied attack in Western Europe would force Hitler to send soldiers away from the Soviet Union. However,

⚠ American soldiers practice loading bombs at a British air base in 1942.

the Allies were not ready. They needed time to prepare. That April, the United States began moving soldiers and supplies to Britain. They would be used for a future invasion of northwestern Europe.

In June, General Dwight D. Eisenhower became the commander of all US forces in Europe. Soon after, US warplanes began taking off from Britain.

They bombed Axis railroads and factories in Western Europe. These attacks hurt Germany's ability to build submarines, airplanes, and other weapons.

The Allies also attacked the Axis forces in North Africa. The Axis powers got most of their oil from North Africa. Oil was needed to make fuel for airplanes, ships, and military vehicles. Cutting off Germany's oil supply hurt its ability to wage war. The Allies also wanted to use bases in North Africa to launch an invasion of Italy. The fight for North Africa ended in May 1943. It was a major Allied victory.

The Allies began the invasion of Italy that July. They started with the island of Sicily. On July 10, the Allies crossed the Mediterranean Sea with 3,000 ships and 150,000 soldiers. Fifteen days later, Mussolini was voted out of power. A new

⚠ An Italian civilian stands outside her ruined home as US soldiers pass through the area.

Italian government was created. It quickly began peace talks with the Allies.

Sicily fell to the Allies on August 17. On September 3, the Allies began invading the Italian mainland. That same day, the Italian government surrendered. A month later, Italy declared war on Germany.

CHAPTER 6

OPERATION OVERLORD

Hitler knew that the Allies would eventually try to invade northwestern Europe. So in 1942, he began building a long line of defenses along the Atlantic coast. The defenses stretched from Norway to Southern France. They included bunkers, **artillery**, and **pillboxes**. Together, the defenses were known as the Atlantic Wall. Hitler believed the Allies would land at Calais,

German soldiers stand guard along the Atlantic coast in occupied France.

France. That is the narrowest point of the English Channel. So, he built the strongest defenses there.

Meanwhile, the Allies were planning an invasion of northwestern Europe. They called it Operation Overlord. Allied leaders chose to land their forces in Normandy, France. Normandy's beaches were an ideal place for troops to land. In addition, Normandy was not as well defended as other places, such as Calais.

The Allies wanted to keep the Germans guessing. So, they built an army of fake tanks and boats in southeastern England. They hoped to trick Germany into thinking the invasion would land at Calais. The trick worked. Germany placed some of its best troops at Calais.

The first day of the invasion was June 6, 1944. It was known as D-Day. In the early morning, Allied paratroopers dropped behind the German

▲ Allied soldiers land on the beaches of Normandy on D-Day.

lines. Their mission was to capture major roads and bridges. At the same time, a fleet of ships crossed the English Channel. These ships carried troops who would storm the beaches.

Thousands of small landing boats brought the Allied soldiers ashore. The soldiers then fought their way up the beaches. German soldiers tried to stop them with machine guns and artillery. More than 4,400 Allied soldiers died. But by the end of the day, the Allies had taken the beaches.

Allied forces then fought their way inland. In western Normandy, soldiers fought in small farm fields. These fields were surrounded by many **hedgerows**. German soldiers fought from behind the thick plants. But the Allies found a way to break through. They put metal blades on the fronts of their tanks. The tanks could then plow through the hedgerows. After two months of fierce fighting, the Allies finally controlled Normandy.

Allied forces entered Paris on August 24. The Germans surrendered the city the next day. One major reason for the Allies' success was that Germany was also fighting the Soviet Union in Eastern Europe. Germany struggled to wage a war on two fronts.

The people of Paris lined the streets to cheer the Allied soldiers. The city had been under Nazi Germany's rule for more than four years. But now it was free.

THE D-DAY LANDINGS

Allied soldiers landed on five beaches on D-Day. The beaches were named Utah, Omaha, Gold, Juno, and Sword.

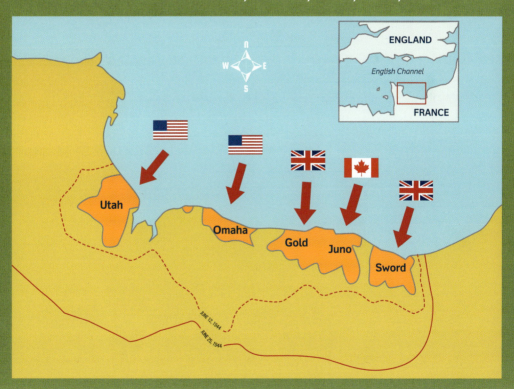

CHAPTER 7

VICTORY IN EUROPE

The Allies reached Germany's western border in early September 1944. This area was heavily defended. Allied leaders sent some of their forces to go around the northern tip of the German defenses. They believed it would be a faster way to enter Germany. Allied paratroopers captured several key towns and bridges in the Netherlands. However, they were driven back by German tanks

The German border was protected by bunkers and concrete tank traps.

and **infantry**. The mission ended in failure for the Allies.

As winter set in, Allied forces stretched approximately 600 miles (1,000 km) around the German border. Many Allied soldiers thought the war would be over soon. Then, on December 16, the Germans launched a major attack. More than 200,000 soldiers and 1,000 tanks fought to drive the Allies out of Europe. Thousands of other German soldiers prepared to join them.

Germany targeted the Forest of Ardennes in Belgium and Luxembourg. German forces pushed the Allies back, creating a bulge in their lines 65 miles (105 km) deep. As a result, the battle became known as the Battle of the Bulge.

Allied soldiers slowed the German advance at the Belgian town of Bastogne. They delayed the Germans long enough for Allied tanks to arrive.

Soldiers dealt with snow and freezing temperatures during the Battle of the Bulge.

The Germans were forced to retreat. The Battle of the Bulge ended on January 25, 1945. It was the largest battle fought on the war's Western Front. Approximately 90,000 Allied soldiers were killed, wounded, or taken prisoner.

By April 1945, the war in Europe was nearly over. However, President Roosevelt did not live to see the end of it. He died suddenly on April 12. Harry S. Truman became the new US president.

The Soviet Union invaded Germany in April. Soviet forces had been fighting the Germans in Eastern Europe since 1941. Now they took the fight into Germany. Both Eisenhower and Stalin wanted their own armies to take Berlin and capture Hitler. However, Eisenhower did not want to lose any more of his soldiers. And he did not want to fight with the Soviets for control of the city. So, Eisenhower agreed to let the Soviets take Berlin.

The Soviets surrounded Berlin in late April. But on April 30, Hitler killed himself rather than be taken prisoner. German forces fought to defend

> **CONSIDER THIS**

Why do you think the United States and the Soviet Union both wanted to capture Berlin?

⚠ The battle for Berlin left much of the city in ruins.

Berlin for another day. However, they surrendered the city on May 2. Five days later, all German forces surrendered.

On May 8, Truman and Churchill made public speeches. They announced that the war in Europe was over. American and British newspapers declared that May 8 was Victory in Europe Day, or V-E Day. However, World War II was not over yet. The war with Japan would go on for several more months.

45

FOCUS ON
WORLD WAR II IN WESTERN EUROPE

Write your answers on a separate piece of paper.

1. Write a paragraph that summarizes the main ideas of Chapter 6.

2. Do you think Roosevelt and Churchill made the correct choice with their "Europe first" plan? Why or why not?

3. Which three countries made up the Axis powers?
   - A. Germany, Denmark, and Belgium
   - B. Germany, Italy, and Japan
   - C. Britain, the United States, and the Soviet Union

4. Which event began World War II?
   - A. Germany invaded the Soviet Union.
   - B. France invaded Germany.
   - C. Germany invaded Poland.

Answer key on page 48.

GLOSSARY

artillery
Large guns, often mounted on wheels.

bunkers
Underground shelters that protect people from falling bombs.

civilians
People who are not in the military.

evacuating
Removing people from a place of danger.

harbors
Calm bodies of water where ships can tie up to the land.

hedgerows
Rows of trees or shrubs that grow around or between fields.

infantry
Soldiers who fight on foot.

occupied
Controlled an area using military power.

phoney
Not real.

pillboxes
Low concrete bunkers with openings for machine guns.

racist
Having to do with hatred or mistreatment of people because of their skin color or ethnicity.

treaty
An official agreement between groups or countries.

TO LEARN MORE

BOOKS

Doeden, Matt. *World War II Resistance Fighters*. Minneapolis: Lerner Publications, 2018.

Mooney, Carla. *Historic Battles from World War II for Kids: 15 Battles from Europe and the Pacific*. Emeryville, CA: Rockridge Press, 2021.

Murray, Laura K. *World War II Technology*. Minneapolis: Abdo Publishing, 2018.

NOTE TO EDUCATORS

Visit www.focusreaders.com to find lesson plans, activities, links, and other resources related to this title.

INDEX

Atlantic, Battle of the, 12–13

Belgium, 16–17, 19, 42
Blitz, 24–25
Britain, Battle of, 23–24

Churchill, Winston, 22, 30, 45

D-Day, 36–38
Denmark, 15
Dunkirk, 17–18

Eisenhower, Dwight D., 31, 44

Hitler, Adolf, 6–7, 9, 16, 18–19, 21–25, 30, 35, 44
Holocaust, 26–27

Japan, 29–30, 45
Jews, 7, 26–27

Mussolini, Benito, 21, 32

Phoney War, 11, 12, 15
Poland, 9–10

Roosevelt, Franklin D., 30, 43

Soviet Union, 25, 30, 38, 44
Stalin, Joseph, 30, 44

Treaty of Versailles, 5–6, 9
Truman, Harry S., 43, 45

Answer Key: 1. Answers will vary; 2. Answers will vary; 3. B; 4. C